You Get What You Believe!

The vital key to abundant

living that most people

never tell you

Rashana

ISBN 978-0-9920307-0-4 (eBook)
ISBN 978-0-9920307-3-5 (Paperback)

Published in Canada by
Inner Nature Publishing

Get One of My Books for Free

How a face reading workshop led to the inspiration to write a book I will never know, but that is how it unfolded. In the summer of 2010, a couple of days after that workshop, I was inspired to gather questions from family and friends and channel the answers to compile into a book. At the time I had been channeling for years but not fully trusting my abilities.

That all changed in the process of writing *Healing with Love, Messages for the New Earth.* Every time I received a question I would channel the answer and send it to the person who submitted the question. The feedback repeatedly was that the message touched them deeply and was very accurate for their life experience. So much love came through that I decided to call it the LoveSpeak Project.

Now, two years later, I call myself a channel and am deeply honoured to have permission to connect with others on such a divine and beautiful level. There are messages in this book that will touch your soul. One question came from a young woman in her 20s who has an untreatable brain tumor. She wanted to know about living so close to death. The answer was one of the most beautiful and moving messages I have ever channeled and it can guide us all when loved ones are close to death.

Other questions were about natural disasters and how to find one's life purpose. It is a diverse collection of messages offered as loving guidance for us all to find our way in this world. I trust that it will touch you as well in some level of your being and I am happy to share it with you.

Get Your Free Copy at www.rashana.ca

Introduction

Little did I know that a year dedicated to healing would lead to the deep understanding that I share with you in this book. I discovered an unseen force at work in our lives pulling us away from our heart's desires. It discreetly infests our thinking and manipulates our actions away from success. It keeps us on the tread mill of life, spinning the past over and over again.

I am so grateful that my journey led me to the life-changing discovery that I share with you in this book. If it was possible to simply think and grow rich, I am sure more of us would have figured it out. We're an intelligent species after all, and who doesn't want to be rich? There is a missing link between your thoughts and your desires that impacts every detail of your life. And it determines success or failure in your ability to make your dreams come true.

Like many great discoveries, I wasn't searching for this information, it found me. My awareness around beliefs came about as an unexpected benefit of my healing work. In my journey I was led to the deep understanding that you get what you believe. I had seen hints of this before, like the statement 'believing is seeing', but I didn't have the deep understanding of how significant our beliefs are.

Every action we take comes from an underlying belief. We can wish for money and joy and happiness for 100 years and never find it if we don't understand the significance of what I share with you here.

This work has made such a difference in my life that I want to share it with you so we can all find the life of our dreams. I can relate to the challenges that many people face in the world today. I was middle aged and unemployed at the time of starting this work. I am now living a life of ease and abundance less than two years later using this material.

If you are ready to learn the missing key to an abundant life read on. If you are not happy with your life it is time to discover how to change it. Until you really understand the impact of your beliefs you won't know how to create your dreams.

Take this journey of discovery with me. Learn how to find the beliefs that are holding you back and how to release them. Only then will you start living the life that you so yearn for. And you deserve it. You simply don't know what is holding you back. I do and I am happy to share it with you. May we all grow and prosper!

Table of Contents

Chapter One - How My Journey Began

The year 2012 was different right from the beginning. I had one word that would describe my focus that year– healing! It was a declaration to the universe that I was ready to do what needed to be done to turn my life around. No more struggling!!! I had been on a spiritual journey for many years and yet, when I looked at my finances and my relationships, life was not improving very much.

I knew that past trauma from my childhood had led me to disassociate from my body. As a child I can only assume it was an effective coping strategy. As an adult, it was keeping me from moving into the fullness of a joyful life.

So on January 6th, the day of my birth, I gifted myself with a soul retrieval. I saw it as a way of bringing all of the pieces of me back that I had left behind in an effort to protect myself as a child. That was how the year started. What came next was beyond anything I would have predicted.

At the time, I was working at a job that was very challenging and I knew I didn't belong there. My vision and my way of being in the world was out of sync with the work environment. Every day I prayed for something different. I did my best to understand what the workplace was showing me. It was a difficult place for me to be – but not for long!

On January 23rd, just a couple of weeks after my soul retrieval, I arrived at work at 8:30 and was gone by 9:00! I was 'released' from my job. I will never forget that day. It was the day of the Chinese New Year, the Year of the Dragon. Another new beginning! I went home, recovered from the shock, and did my happy dance! I fully understood that the universe had given me just what I had asked for.

My friends told me I should dispute the job loss. My reply was, that would be like asking for an ice-cream cone, getting an ice-cream cone, and then complaining because I got an ice-cream cone. I had been asking for a change and the universe gave me a change. It didn't look the way I thought it would, but it was what I asked for.

I love the way the universe lines things up. Just eight days before the 'release' from my job I had attended a workshop that helped me identify what I truly wanted to be doing at that point in my life. What revealed itself was that I wanted to be developing and facilitating workshops. As I said, I was unhappy in my job but not expecting any sudden changes. I believe that the identification of what I truly wanted to be doing was the perfect preparation for the news I had just received.

Perhaps it was that awareness that guided me to make a conscious decision to stay positive and not step into fear around all that was happening. All change leads to something better. That was my new mantra. Every time I found my mind wanting to wander into the 'what if's' I overrode it and faithfully repeated, all change leads to something better.

Little did I know how often I would get to use this mantra! Just six weeks after being freed from my job the universe sent another whopper my way. It was now March. I was at my computer, opened my inbox and there was an email from my landlord. He regretted to advise that he was selling the condo I was living in and I had to move!

Now I have to admit that my mantra went out the window for a couple of hours while I contemplated just what the heck was going on in my life! But I didn't give myself much time to linger there.

I quickly returned to 'all change leads to something better', repeating that over and over to myself. As I wondered what that 'something better' might be, it came to me. I was free to live wherever I wanted. I didn't have to stay in the city because I wasn't tied down to a job or a lease. I was free!

Between January 28th when my job ended and mid-March when I learned I had to move, my personal healing journey had already started. A former Reiki student of mine resurfaced into my life. He was practicing Theta Healing and was doing work with me around my family. Of course, family is a great place to begin our healing journey.

We have parents, siblings and other relatives who all have played a role in instituting some of the unhealthy beliefs that we carry within our subconscious. I think it was because I had done this healing work that, when thinking about where I would like to move to, I immediately thought of the small university town I lived in over 30 years ago.

I had always loved the town and it would place me closer to family. It truly is an amazing life when we pay attention to all the synchronicities. Just two days before learning about the condo selling I had decided that I wanted to be living closer to nature. I didn't give it much thought – it was just a feeling. On hind sight, I realize it also helped me prepare for leaving the city and moving to the small town that I now call home.

I have been pretty much a nomad since leaving home at 18. In the years leading up to this moment, I have moved almost every single year. My record is 3 years in the same house. That leads to another incredible unfolding of 2012. On June 1st, when I settled into my new apartment, in this little town that I have always been drawn to, I felt like I was truly home for the first time in my life!

I may not stay in this apartment forever but I know I will always call this town home. Through my willingness to accept the changes that were unfolding in my life, I learned to have faith and to trust the changes that life always brings. Combined with the benefits of the healing work, I started living from a place of purpose instead of living from fear.

What all of this has taught me is that every step we take is influenced by our thoughts and/or beliefs. I am now living what I know to be my soul purpose. I am offering workshops, just like I discovered I wanted to be doing before losing my job. I am offering sound healing which I have been using in my own practice since the year 2000. I am living in a way that nourishes my soul.

I don't do what I love, I do what I Am! By dedicating my year to healing and deciding to look for the best possible outcome with every experience that came my way, I changed the probable outcome of my life from one of hardship to great joy. It didn't happen without commitment and a lot of work.

My healing continued all year, right into December when I finally received a deeper soul retrieval with my beautiful friend who was at my side supporting me every step of the way. At times the healing work was so intense I felt like my finger was plugged into a socket. Every release meant that my body was shifting and changing.

I know it was my commitment to healing that brought this friend into my life to support me through that journey. And it was my determination to get it done that kept me on track, even when the work was challenging. The rewards are immeasurable. Life just continues to offer more support as I release more and more of the old beliefs that would have kept me from my true expression in this world.

And now I invite you to journey with me as I offer you the understanding and the tools that will help you come to the same place in your own life. Join me as I support you in finding your deepest truth by releasing the beliefs that keep you from loving yourself. This is the key to moving forward and creating the life you have always yearned for.

On the other side is joy, mystery and celebration. Life is meant to be a beautiful discovery – a discovery of the full potential of you and all the rewards that follow. What I realize from my year of healing is that we often repeat the familiar patterns of the past and our lives never change.

In order to find the fullness of who we are under the wounded self, we have to commit to looking at the pain and the patterns that we mindlessly repeat over and over. Without awareness of what these are, we will keep repeating the patterns of our past instead of becoming who we truly are.

I will let you know right now that it takes courage and commitment to do this work. In order to begin clearing the beliefs about ourselves that are not fully loving, we need to be willing to look at the painful hidden aspects of who we are that we don't like to admit to. If you insist that everything is good and there is nothing to work on and yet you are not happy, you are deceiving only yourself.

You wouldn't be reading this book if you weren't looking for something. The more you incorporate what is offered here into your life the more positive changes you will see you in your experience. We see what we believe. Everything in our life experience comes from our beliefs. We create what we believe we deserve. Many people will say, "I certainly didn't believe I deserve this mess" and yet, with exploration, it will be discovered that their beliefs did indeed bring every life experience to them.

Because so many of our beliefs are subconscious we don't have an awareness of the foundation that we are creating our lives from. I learned this over and over in 2012. Every time I felt a fear or concern about anything I realized that there was a subconscious belief influencing my thinking.

Through exploration I was able to discover what the belief was. Once identified, I would use the tools I will be sharing with you here to release it, so that my response to life would no longer come from a place of limitation.

The more we do this, the fuller life becomes. As we love ourselves more we create a life that reflects that love. Hardship and despair are created from not loving the self; we don't *believe* we deserve a good life even though that is what we want. Those unconscious beliefs impact us without any awareness of it and yesterday keeps repeating over and over and over.

For those who are ready for change, read on. I will be taking you onto a journey of self-discovery that has the potential to lead to a life of joy, grace and abundance. As you identify and release the hidden beliefs that are holding you back, you then have the potential to live life from a place of real love and happiness.

It is my great delight to share this system of change with you. Each person who does the work to heal will respond to the world more from a place of love. As that grows, the world becomes a more loving place. For those of us who are sensitive to all the pain and hardship in the world, this is a very real and tangible way to make a change not only in our own lives, but in the lives of all those around us.

As we change, so must our family change. As our family changes, so must the community surrounding it change. And on it goes. This is my vision in sharing this work with you. With every clearing you do, you fall deeper into a state of peace. I'll meet you there on this beautiful journey that we call life.

Deliverance

Oh tired my weary eyes, for they do not see
the truth.
They weep at the deception of pain and
suffering.
Their burden weights my heart with the
delusion of despair.
Lift me above my imagined reality.
Show me the truth so that I may be free.
It is only a game we are playing to assist
each other in the illusion.
Let us see the TRUTH and change the rules.
We do not suffer ~ we choose.
I now choose a joyous life.
I choose prosperity and abundance.
I choose love.
The Love of Creator fills my soul ~ my heart,
and I laugh.
I laugh at my folly.
I laugh at my forgetfulness.
I AM the Light. I radiate forth each day to
illumine all those who stand before me.
My spark is ignited.
I AM.

Chapter Two - You Are a Prisoner to Your Hidden Beliefs

I often say we have a childhood so that we have something to work on as adults. Really, I don't know anyone who made it through childhood unscathed. It's part of the process of the human journey.

This awareness is not about blaming our parents or caregivers for their role in our development. They were doing the best they could with what they knew from their own life experience. The problem arises when we don't realize that we are carrying hidden baggage around that is influencing our decisions as adults. As a result, we live the same life year after year – each day the same as the last – or worse, each day is more miserable than the last.

I recently ran into a friend that I hadn't seen in about five years. We decided to meet for coffee a few days later. As we were catching up I realized it was like no time had passed, because she was sharing the same story I had heard the last time I saw her. In the big picture nothing had changed. She still had the same money concerns and complaints about her husband. Five years had passed and yet her life story was very much the same.

It was an interesting opportunity for me to see how much my life had changed. With my dedication to healing and allowing myself to grow I was sharing a new story, not the one she had heard from me the last time we saw each other.

This was validated another time not long before that. A friend who I hadn't seen in probably ten years called me out of the blue. She was just chatting and sharing what was going on in her life. Once again I realized that it sounded like the same story from ten years previous.

This friend is very intuitive. As I was listening attentively to her sharing about her life she suddenly said, "You feel so clear. Good for you" and then she quickly hung up. If I hadn't done my healing work I would have jumped right into her story with my own complaints about how miserable life was, wondering when it would ever change!

Some people go to their grave carrying their childhood wounds, never fully understanding the impact it has on their lives. They deserve a medal because it's not easy holding onto all our anger and sadness and fear. And even worse, it keeps us from ever achieving the life of happiness that we so deserve.

All the wounds from our past – our baggage – are carried in the subconscious. Think of the subconscious as a giant suitcase that is storing all the beliefs that you developed in order to protect yourself in the past. Small children are totally dependent on their parents or caregivers to provide for them and keep them safe. To a child who cannot rationally reason life circumstances, the smallest thing can feel like a threat to survival and so children develop a variety of coping strategies.

For example, I developed the belief that if I express my anger, or any of my feelings really, I will be rejected. Perhaps there was a moment in my childhood where I expressed anger and was reprimanded for it and so I learned or believed that it's not safe to be angry. That belief then influenced my life in ways that I wasn't aware of.

In my marriage I would never express my true feelings. I thought being a good person was turning the other cheek and putting my needs aside. The outcome was that I finally felt so unsupported that I left the marriage – much to the surprise of my partner. He never learned just how unhappy I was because I was afraid to express it. That is only one example of how our hidden beliefs can impact our lives without us being aware.

In keeping with this, I can safely say that every single person who has any issues around money has hidden beliefs that are keeping them from their abundance. The challenge is that these beliefs are deeply buried and therefore, until we make a conscious decision to look for them, they hold us back from receiving an abundant life.

Every time you have a fear about money you can be sure there is an underlying belief that is the foundation to that fear. Some people have trouble accepting this fact. They may say, "Yes I have fear about paying my bills because the money isn't there."

They don't realize that there is a link between the money not being there and an underlying belief somewhere that they don't deserve it, or they have to work hard for it, or there is never enough. Something is there creating the experience of not enough money. Without awareness, the pattern just keeps repeating. It's just that simple.

There are a lot of books and speakers who tell us we need to change our thinking in order to change our lives. I do believe this is true. However, they are missing a fundamental key to this process. It is much harder to change your thinking into having money when there is a deeply entrenched belief that you don't have money and your life is proving it!

The important step that is missing for most people is before you can 'think' abundance and achieve it, you must identify the core belief that has you living in lack. Only after clearing that subconscious belief will your thinking shift to abundance. When approached in this way, everything switches. Life starts to offer opportunities instead of lack after the clearing has happened.

Let me give you an example of how powerful this can be. My story is related to abundance but not necessarily money, although I have done a lot of work around my money beliefs as well. Much of my life I had felt like I was alone in this world with no true support from others.

This appeared most acutely when I would travel alone. I once went on a trade mission to Germany. Even though I was with a group of people, I didn't really connect with any of them. When it came time to meet people to promote my product I was taken to city center by one of the support staff and left there with the names of a few stores to contact. My support person went back to the office and I was left in a foreign country on my own.

Then, a few days later, I was put on a train by myself to go to Austria to promote myself at a holistic fair. Again, I was alone. Other people in the same trade mission were escorted and chauffeured and I was sent off on my own. What I now realize is that my beliefs created this experience. The support staff had arranged for a translator for me in Austria and I did my best to say I didn't need a translator even though I felt alone and unsupported. I was feeling like I had no support and at the same time refusing support! The irony wasn't so clear to me at the time!

This story is fresh in my mind because it was only recently that I identified this core belief and cleared it. I was on day three of a major headache and I finally gave in – after thinking I could do this on my own (there's that belief) – and called my friend who I mentioned previously for some healing and releasing work.

What I realized in conversation with him was that the headache was triggered by recent plans to travel on my own. This brought up memories of the past trip to Germany which I now recognized as beliefs about being alone and unsupported. This time I was still going to be in Canada but the fear of travelling on my own was there.

The headache was a blessing in disguise. It was so painful that I gave in and asked for help. After we cleared my underlying belief of being unsupported in the world, the shift was incredible. Support started showing up everywhere. The following day I was doing a presentation about sound healing which I use in my healing practice. I said during the talk that I would like to be doing sounding at the local children's hospital and the woman in the front row, who I had been making eye contact with during the talk, spoke right up and said, "I'm a nurse there. I can help you with that" and she took my card after my presentation.

The next day I was giving a workshop and there was a couple who attended who had booked a channeling session after the workshop. It turned out that no one was booked for a half hour after their session and so we had lots of time to talk. In the conversation they told me that they do work online and would like to help me promote my business!

I had not asked or even hinted at asking for support and there it was! For the following two days after that I had similar experiences. Support just kept falling out of the sky and landing in my lap. That is how quickly things can change when we change our subconscious beliefs.

All my life I had been held back by a belief that I didn't even know I had. That is why I say we are prisoners to our beliefs. We do so much work to move forward and get what we desire in life. We work harder, learn more, repeat affirmations and observe our thoughts. These are all important pieces of creating a new life, but until the hidden beliefs of the subconscious are released, we are their prisoner.

All the time we think our logical mind is in control of our lives when it is not. It is responding to the subconscious that is on automatic pilot to repeat what was, based on past experiences. The incredible shift that I experienced from not being supported to allowing support into my life clearly shows how this works.

This is why we must be willing to dig in and release our core beliefs that are no longer serving us. Until we do, we keep creating life experiences that show us our beliefs of lack or whatever it is that we are creating.

All we have to do is look at our lives to have some sense of where we are in this regard. What are the issues that keep repeating in your life? They will show you some of the core beliefs that are there influencing your daily decisions. As adults we don't need to be living under the limitations of our beliefs that hold us back.

This is why it is so fundamental to search into the subconscious and release all that is holding you back from living the life you yearn for. The greatest gift you can give yourself is the commitment to do this work and stop subconsciously sabotaging your efforts to create abundance, joy, peace and whatever else you desire in your life.

I AM

Let the thunder roll in your mind like the hills
tumbling from the mountain.
Let the resounding vibration fill your essence
and awaken you to that which you truly are; a
God force in dormancy, beginning to awaken.
Let the thunder roll in your mind like waves in
the ocean crashing to shore ~ reaching their
destination.
Let it awaken you so that you may be in truth
~ no longer living the illusion.
The dream is over. You are in charge now.
Let the thunder roll and awaken you to your I
AM.
I AM the thunder in the air.
I AM the water in the ocean.
I AM the Love of God in the heart of a child.
I AM the essence of all that is.
I AM the gift that God has given itself,
therefore I shall be all that I came to be.

Chapter Three - Why You Must do Releasing Work to Start Living Your Best Life

In the last chapter you learned that unconscious beliefs can sabotage your life. Because they are unconscious, you are not aware that they are holding you back. They continue to influence your life and you repeat the same patterns over and over.

So how do you break the cycle? You do it with intention and determination to move through your limiting beliefs and find your way to a fulfilling life. Until you are willing to look into the shadows you will not find what is lurking there.

Many people resist doing this work because they are afraid of what they will find or they think it will be too hard. As long as you are afraid to dig deep and see the truth that lies in the shadows you will respond from those fearful thoughts and just keep repeating the life you are already living.

I know you are reading this because you would like to see changes in your life. At times it may seem easier to ignore what is and keep living the way you have been, but the truth is it takes a lot of energy to worry about things and hold onto the patterns that keep your life on repeat.

The mind is constantly rolling over the 'what ifs', eluded away from stillness or peace. It takes much more energy to hold onto those limiting beliefs and fears than it does to release them. So why do we try so hard to hang onto them? We hang on so tightly because our beliefs were created as methods of survival.

As children, when we feel threatened by a situation or person, we find ways to protect ourselves. Sometimes that means being very quiet and not seen, so we keep all our thoughts and feelings inside. Sometimes we act aggressively – pushing people and opportunities away so we are guaranteed not to be hurt again.

Sometimes, like my story about receiving support, we feel like we have to take care of ourselves and do it alone so we push support away. Are you seeing the irony here? The very methods we use to protect ourselves keep us from receiving the thing we are protecting ourselves from.

As a child I needed to believe that I could take care of myself and manage everything on my own because I did not receive support when I needed it or cried out for it. As an adult, that belief then kept me from allowing people to support me. Until I cleared it, being unsupported was my experience. I continued to feel like I was an island, fending for myself with no one to lean on. I am so grateful that I found that hidden belief because releasing it has certainly changed my life.

Another example that is so common in our world is the belief that we never have enough money. When we hold that subconscious belief we actually create situations that make sure we never have enough money. This was clear to me one day when I was in conversation with a family member. She told me she had given up on saving money because every time she got just a little money in the bank, something would happen and she would have to spend it. The car would break down or an appliance would need to be replaced. What most people don't realize is that there is a connection to the subconscious, limiting beliefs and the life situations that come about as a result of those beliefs. As long as we believe, somewhere in our subconscious, that we never have money, we will unwittingly create circumstances that show up as not having money.

I know this can sound unbelievable but I assure you it is the way it works. You can ignore this truth and keep on living the same experiences you have already been living, like my friend I hadn't seen in five years, or you can try what I am sharing in this book and see if anything changes. Like everything else, you see what you believe!

If all this is true, which I assure you it is, then you might be wondering why we resist changing our beliefs so much. It is because they were set up as a form of protection. Changing them can feel like our very survival is threatened when we think of letting them go. As adults, in most cases, we no longer need to use our childhood survival techniques. We are capable of taking care of ourselves.

Yet, even though we are no longer dependent on someone else to provide for us, we still carry around our dysfunctional survival tools that influence every action we take. Letting go of them can be very scary. We may feel like we will die without them and so we hang on tight, keeping them close to our hearts. The irony is that in order to live a full, abundant and joyful life we must let these defenses die. We must be willing to go to the place of vulnerability and release the dysfunctional defenses that keep us from creating the beautiful life that we so deserve.

I believe that one of the most courageous things we can do in our lives is to allow ourselves to be vulnerable. Society teaches us that it is not acceptable to show feelings or appear weak in any way. We even shun away from death, treating it like another shadow that is to be avoided at all cost.

We see death as vulnerability and we run from it with all we've got. In truth some kind of death is required to transition to another level of being. And the death of our limiting beliefs is just another example of that.

In order to find life on the other side of our limiting beliefs we must allow something to die and we must allow ourselves to be vulnerable enough to let it happen. As long as we are still walking around with our wall of defenses solidly built, we will not let anyone tear it down so that we can open our hearts once again.

It is from a loving heart that we create lives full of joy and abundance. That love must be for ourselves. Many people are loving to others but not capable of receiving anything for themselves. This is not a healthy form of love. It is needy love. We are loving and kind to others because we want them to like us and accept us.

It is actually our fear of not being loved that drives us to be so loving in this instance. In order to allow abundance to flow into our lives, we must love ourselves enough to receive it. A person who does not believe they deserve love will not allow love to come to them.

As well, they won't allow all the things that represent love to come to them, like relationships, money to live a full life and so on. Until such a person heals the belief that they are unlovable, these patterns will repeat in their life over and over and over. All the while they will be wondering why things never improve.

"I am a good person" they will say, thinking they deserve more. And they do deserve more, they just don't believe it. They think it, but in some core place in their being they do not believe it, and that is the difference.

Have you ever known someone who you would consider not a very nice person yet they have lots of money? This is proof that it takes more than being a nice person to allow money into your experience. Have you ever known someone who works their way up the ladder in business even though they know less than the people who work under them?

This proves that it takes more than skill to have financial success. What these people have is the belief that they deserve to be rich and successful. They believe in themselves therefore their life experience must meet that belief. I have met people who have lots of money yet they are ruthless and disrespectful.

I used to wonder why that was. I felt like the universe was playing some kind of cruel trick on me. I am a good person after all. Somehow I believed that being a good person should be enough to equate riches and success. If only it were that simple. It didn't happen until I did lots of healing work. I had to release many levels of beliefs that wouldn't allow me to receive or love myself.

Take a moment to look at the people in your life experience who seem to have what you are looking for even though they are not exceptional people in any way. Take note of their attitude about themselves. Would you say they love themselves and believe that they deserve to be where they are?

It may not be a healthy love, it may be narcissistic, but it is their love of self and the belief that they deserve what they have that allows them be in the position they are in. If you want to have what they have, you have to get to the deep seated belief that you deserve to have it. If there are any feelings of vengeance or jealousy against those who have money and success then you are not believing that you deserve it.

It is only when you can appreciate what the rich and successful have created in their lives, and know that you deserve the same, that you are beginning to find your way to it. Resentment of any kind means you have hidden beliefs that keep you from knowing that you can have the same.

You will know that you have healed your subconscious beliefs when you can appreciate the gift they have given you. For example, for most of my life I was not able to connect to people on a truly personal level. I was always outside of my body so to speak. When I was in school I would always sleep on the school bus so that I wouldn't have to be in conversation with anyone.

The need to disconnect from people was a survival technique from my childhood but it was keeping me from fulfilling experiences in my adulthood. When I finally realized what I was doing and cleared the beliefs that had me living that way, I was grateful for the experience.

I realized that, for most of my life, I was more connected with the spiritual aspect of myself than the physical body experience. From that I developed intuitive abilities that are a large part of my work. I have the honour of connecting with people on a soul level and may not have developed those abilities if it weren't for my coping strategies. Once I could appreciate that my tendency to be out of body led to my intuitive skills, I knew the success of my healing around that experience.

The more healing you do, the more you see what else wants to be cleared. It is like letting a crack of light into a dark space, it wants to illuminate the whole room. Once we begin this journey of healing, new aspects of ourselves will come to the surface so that we can continue releasing and growing.

The more we are willing to become a new person, relieved of the old patterns that held us prisoner to what was, the more limiting beliefs will surface for clearing. It is an ongoing cycle but it gets easier and easier to clear.

As well, what surfaces is going deeper and deeper into the psyche so that our lives become more joyful as we do the work. The more burdens we release the easier life becomes. I now walk through life from a place of great contentment and stillness. This in itself is abundance and to me it is the greatest reason to be doing this work.

The Eyes of Love

The eyes of love look upon your Soul like
the sun awakening the dawn of a new day.
The eyes of love look into your heart to
witness the beauty that lies within.
The eyes of love reveal your pain with
understanding and compassion.
Look carefully and see the glory of who you
are,
for the eyes of love have no judgement.

Chapter Four - How I Went from Unhappy and Unemployed at 56 to Abundant at 57

You have already heard a good part of my story. 2012 was the year that my life turned around. What could have resulted in hardship was turned into opportunity for two reasons: one, because I was willing to look at everything very differently than I had in the past (responding out of love instead of fear) and two, because I was releasing the hidden beliefs that would have otherwise held me prisoner to them.

Life situations, or circumstances, always come to us as an opportunity for growth. Every part of our life experience is created by the higher aspect of our soul as an opportunity to move into something new. If we respond the way we always have, we repeat the past until we finally realize that something needs to change.

That is what this human experience is all about. Until we understand that our life experiences are opportunities to grow and release, the same kind of experiences will keep repeating in our lives. They will continue to show up, over and over until we get it.

Little did I know that my dedication to healing was me 'getting it'. Throughout the year, every time I felt a fear around something I would call my friend and we would clear it. For example, I was scheduled to be part of a program for new businesses starting up. The program provides a certain amount of funds while you develop your business.

For me it would provide enough to cover my monthly rent, phone and car expenses. Without that support I would be looking for a job instead of establishing my business. When I lost my job I truly understood that I was being given a new opportunity to start over doing what I was passionate about and knew to be my life purpose. This program would allow me to do that. One of the requirements of the program was that no business was to be conducted before starting and you couldn't be employed and be accepted into the program. It was a waiting game between the time of applying to the program and learning that you are accepted and starting the program.

At the time of my application I was receiving unemployment benefits. It was a minimal monthly income – just enough to meet my expenses with about $50 for groceries every week. I gave up my cell phone, put my student loan on hold and I was able to get by.

However, those benefits were due to run out very soon. If I didn't get accepted into the self-employment program I would be left looking for a job from a place of desperation because I would have no income. During the period of waiting I started to become fearful that I wouldn't be accepted and I would be left scrambling at the last minute to find a job. At 56, living in a small town where I knew very few people, that looked a little scary.

Recognizing that my fearful thinking could lead to creating the very experience I was hoping to avoid, I took the steps to dig into the shadows of the fear and find out what was going on. I called my friend. This one was deep. It took him an hour on the phone to convince me that what I was feeling was really an aspect of my ego. I am so grateful that he was willing to stay with me, digging and digging until we got to the treasure of the hidden belief.

Thankfully I did get accepted into the program. The interesting thing is, a few weeks after starting, I received a call from the worker who had approved the initial application and sent it on for processing. She had learned that several people who had initially been told they would be accepted into the program had found at the last minute that there weren't enough funds and their applications were rejected.

I knew in that moment that I could have been one of those people. If I had not identified the core beliefs that were creating the fears of not being approved I am certain that I would have also received the bad news. Of course there is no proof of this but I have done enough of this work to see the results of clearing limiting beliefs.

I am also very intuitive and I believe the reason that I started to doubt that I would be accepted is because I was picking up on the potential of a negative outcome. I would like to add that, at 56, not only did I fall into the 'mature' category to be looking for employment, I was also single, with no savings what-so-ever and no family member who could jump in and support me financially.

I was on my own (which, in hindsight is no surprise since I hadn't released the belief of being unsupported). You can see that I had a history around money. There were deep beliefs that needed to be cleared in order for me to accept prosperity into my life.

What I have learned in this process is that all our hidden beliefs affect all aspects of our lives. For example, that belief around receiving support was part of receiving abundance as well. Once I stopped believing that I had to do everything on my own, people started showing up who were not only supporting me, but their support was helping me receive abundance.

And that is how this story comes to the present. Before clearing the limiting belief that I had to do everything on my own and walk through life with no support, I realized that the greatest potential for me to expand my business was by tapping into the world-wide market, using the Internet to promote my work.

Thanks to Skype I could offer sessions online. However, I am not too computer savvy and not too fond of teaching myself how to do things on the computer. I get frustrated because my knowledge is so limited that every step seems to take a long time. Here's the beauty of this releasing work.

As I briefly mentioned, two days after clearing my belief around support, a woman attending one of my workshops offered to help me with online marketing! She had no idea that I wanted to do that. She had only met me that day, but she saw my skills and wanted to help. And she made her living with online marketing!

How does it get any better than that? This, to me, is when it starts to feel magical – when we do the clearing work and immediately things shift. If we are willing and clear enough to receive it, life begins to flow with ease and grace.

With my new friend's support my life turned around. I already had a variety of products and had written a few books. I just didn't have the marketing skills to bring them to the world. I now find myself doing the work that I absolutely love to do. Life is full and rich and joyous and abundant.

Not to say that all the healing work is done. My philosophy is that when we are finished doing our 'work' we check out. That is, things will continue to find their way to the surface as long as we are walking and breathing on this planet. But it gets easier and easier.

After a while even the challenges are welcomed because you know that it is an opportunity to clear more hidden beliefs. Life actually starts to be fun because you get to see the huge synchronicities that line up once the limiting beliefs are released.

I am now living a full life and the journey to that is what I am offering you in this book. This will be the beginning and the tools that I am giving here will get you started. If you find that you need support in this healing work, I would advise a practitioner of Theta Healing or Access Consciousness or some other method of healing that releases hidden beliefs from the subconscious.

You may do that work with me if you choose. More information about my Release Technique is listed at the end of the book. The choice is yours. You may find that you are able to do the work that you need using the tools offered here.

Just know that some of those beliefs are so deeply buried that it can be difficult to find them. Whatever your decision, I invite you to dedicate the next several months to this journey of discovery knowing that, on the other side, life just keeps getting better and better.

Autumn

The summer fades now . . . her blossoms
shiver,
awaiting the morning light;
the drone is lost to the chill of clarity.
A new time is beginning.
Go within now . . .
join the trees in their silent meditation;
transit with them into the darkness.
Prepare for the great awakening
that will come again with spring.

Chapter Five - Find It and Free It

So far I have discussed why it is necessary to work on your beliefs. Releasing limiting beliefs will lead to the place of allowing a joyous and abundant life. Now let's start to look at how that happens. This is the stage where you have to be like a detective, picking up on every clue that you can find that leads to discovering what your beliefs really are.

Like I said, sometimes they are well hidden because we have a secret caretaker called the ego. As human beings, we all have an ego. It does what it can to keep us safe. Very often, to the ego, that means doing what we have always done. It worked before so why not do it again the ego says. This repeats over and over until we have deeply entrenched patterns in our brains.

The ego can comfortably say, when I face this experience, this is how I respond. Anything else can be terrifying. The ego loves to stay with the familiar. That is why making change is so challenging. I am asking you (and your ego) to step into the unknown – the unfamiliar!

"Run for your lives" the ego says. "This is not how we handle this situation. No, no, no. We bury our head in the sand and cover our ears." And that voice of the ego is very convincing. It also brings the body on board. We've all felt the physical reactions to fear. Our heart races and our stomach turns as every part of our being puts up resistance.

Remember we talked about death before. Every time we want to grow in our lives, or become someone new, a piece of the old self has to die to make room for the new self. We have to be willing to forget who we were in order to become who we truly are.

It can be very fearful to walk through these solid beliefs and do something different. Remember, these beliefs were set up in the first place as a form of protection. Now I am asking you to let go of that protection. From what we have learned so far we know that the protection we set up as children or in earlier life circumstances, doesn't serve our present experience. It keeps us from getting what we truly desire to have.

But, the ego has our minds and bodies trained to respond in a certain way and therefore we step into fear at the thought of doing anything different. Not only are we changing our mental responses to situations with this work, but we also have to be aware that our bodies are on automatic response as well.

Our life circumstances are held within every cell of our body. Every cell stores memory of the past. I have heard stories of people receiving organ transplants and then suddenly craving different foods or having memories that they never had before. This is proof to me that the cells of the donor have memories.

It is my belief that all illness has an emotional foundation. The cells of our bodies respond to our thoughts and beliefs. If they are fearful thoughts and beliefs then the body shrinks up and doesn't allow the life force to flow through. And the opposite is also true.

Did you ever know someone who was happy all the time? Did that person ever get sick? In my experience the answer is no. Happiness is health. Fear is illness. This also relates to the clearing work. Once you have cleared the belief, the body also needs to learn that it is OK to respond differently to the experience and release the fear as well.

It's important to be aware of this as you move forward. You may find buried beliefs and release them only to find that the next time you face a similar circumstance the body still responds in fear.

Once I became aware of this cellular memory I realized that even though I had cleared beliefs around a certain situation, my body would still send out fear based reactions that would try to keep me from moving fully into my desire. An example is related to my fear of being alone when travelling.

I cleared the beliefs based on finances and support around travel, but I noticed my body still held some fear. Simply recognizing that gave me the courage to move forward and teach the body that this time everything is OK. It is important to get back on the horse after falling off so to speak. That means that, when we have a negative experience, it need only happen once for the body to remember it and not want to repeat that experience.

If we push ourselves through a similar experience when we know there will be a positive outcome, then we can retrain the body to expect a different outcome – a positive outcome. The sooner we do this the better. The longer our body stores a negative memory, the more it gets affirmed without us even realizing it. Sometimes our reactions are so subconscious we are not even aware that we are repeating the fearful response.

When looking for our unconscious patterns, the real challenge is in finding the limiting beliefs. After all, they are hidden! How do we uncover them so that we can use the tools to change them? The answer is to know where they are peeping through into our reality. Basically they come from a body response or a thought response to any situation.

Recognizing it in the body is easier than the thoughts. Once we start to pay attention to the body we can see when it is responding with fear. The solar plexus is the area of the body that is connected to the subconscious. It is the area of the diaphragm. When we have a sick feeling there, it is often fear. It is considered our power center. If we are in a power struggle with someone we will feel it in the solar plexus. It is our more primitive intuitive center where the fight or flight response comes from.

Often when I am releasing fear I feel it leaving in that part of the body. It is like a sick feeling in my gut. I have come to recognize it as fear releasing. Another way that my body releases is to sigh. Because I have done so much clearing work I often will have a big sigh during a conversation with someone and I know that something just got released – usually for both of us!

Once we become aware, we can recognize when the body is responding from hidden beliefs and also when it is releasing. It is important to pay attention to the body because it is giving valuable clues as to what is going on in your internal world.

The body's more visceral responses to situations are often easier to recognize than our thoughts. The shadow self is the part of ourselves that we like to keep in the dark. It is the aspects of ourselves that we don't want to see. It is easy to notice behaviours in others that we don't like or approve of.

Admitting that we have those same qualities of character ourselves is a more challenging task. Even though many of us are very good at putting ourselves down or demanding more of ourselves, there are still pieces that remain hidden. For example, if I am always judging others for being stupid, it may be very hard for me to see where I believe that I am stupid.

On the outside I have little tolerance for stupidity so I certainly wouldn't think that I have that belief about myself, but the truth is that it must be there somewhere, hidden within the subconscious or it wouldn't bother me. This is what is meant by the shadow side. And this is the challenge of doing this work. We have to be willing to have a look into the shadows and pull out the beliefs that are lurking there.

Here is a statement that I want you to consider because it is fundamental to this work. You may be starting to realize this from what I have written so far. EVERYTHING IN OUR EXTERNAL WORLD COMES FROM OUR THOUGHTS and BELIEFS. E v e r y t h i n g.

What we see on the outside is a reflection of what we believe on the inside. If we are going to 'Find It', that is, if we are going to find the hidden patterns that create our everyday reality, we have to understand this concept. Everything that happens in the world travels through our filters. That is why five people can witness an accident and everyone will have a different version of what happened.

Again, we see what we believe. If you were in an accident when you were a child, it may trigger memories that take you back to the time of your initial trauma. That memory will filter what you just witnessed and you might give a whole different version of the accident than someone standing beside you.

We always respond from our personal experience. And this is true for all the relationships we have in the world. That would include the co-worker you hate, your child that you love, your motorbike that makes you feel free and your sore toe that holds you back. All of it comes from your thinking which is based on your beliefs.

Remember what I shared about releasing my belief about not being supported in life and how the support started showing up the very next day! I assure you that was no coincidence. Once we start believing something new, something new can show up in our reality.

As long as we believe what we have always believed, our reality will be what it has always been. Nothing will change. Look at your own life and explore this for yourself. The reason that it is important to understand this is that you won't be willing to look at the shadow side of yourself to find the hidden gems if you don't understand how this works.

It takes courage to look at the parts of yourself that you don't particularly like and accept them as part of who you are. The reason you don't see them is because you don't want to admit that you have those qualities. And yet, whether you accept it or not, those qualities and beliefs are impacting your life.

I think it is better to have a good look inside and release what you can, than continue to run from your shadows and never find the joy you so deeply yearn for. As long as you are running, the shadows will chase you. Once you have the courage to stop, turn around and face them, they begin to disappear. This may not happen all in one go, but the more you are willing to look inside, the clearer you become.

And every time you face something that is chasing you, your life feels lighter and easier. You're not running quite so fast or so hard. And then you start to notice that good things are happening and there is more peace. Eventually you get to the point where you celebrate the hardships that come into your experience because you know it's another great opportunity to release one more hidden thought system that no longer serves your highest potential!

One of the easiest ways to find our shadows or hidden beliefs is to look at our judgement of others. Judgement shows up in our lives in two ways – what we like and what we don't like about others. Let's start with an example based on what we like.

Every time you give someone a compliment, like "I love your sweater", what you are really saying is I would like to have that sweater because I think it would look great on me. What you are seeing in the other person that you are complimenting them on is what you would like for yourself.

Let's take this a step deeper. When you compliment someone for being so organized, you see in them the part of yourself that appreciates organization. Because you admire that trait, you compliment the person on it. Another example is when we say someone has good taste.

What we are really saying is that they like what we like. If we think about someone who we think has bad taste, it means that we don't like what they like. We generalize it by saying they have bad taste, but according to whose standards? Ours. Undoubtedly *they* think they have good taste! Think about someone you complimented lately so you can find the truth in this for yourself. The more you understand this, the better it will work for you.

Now, let's look at the flip side of this. When we see something in another person that we don't like we judge them. For example, maybe you think your co-worker is lazy and doesn't do her share of the work. She always seems to be sitting around and if you ask her to do something she has a reason why she can't do it.

You get frustrated with this and eventually start daydreaming about her quitting so that someone more competent could take her place. Here's where the truth comes in. Just like giving a compliment is seeing something in the other person that we like about ourselves, having a judgement of someone else is really judging that characteristic in *ourselves* that we don't like.

This time we have to ask the same kind of questions, only it is looking at the shadow side – the traits we don't want to admit to. Have you ever heard the saying everyone is a mirror for us? Everyone in our life experience is showing us something about ourselves. What a great opportunity to see who we truly are – if we are willing to look!

So, in the case of the lazy co-worker, the question you need to ask is, where am I lazy? Where do I resist doing my work? "Now hold on!" you might say. "The reason I dislike that person being lazy is because I am ambitious. There is nothing lazy about me." And my response would be "Let's do a little exploring."

If you are having trouble identifying in yourself what you judge about others, ask your friends for help. Ask them outright, "Do you ever see parts of me that are lazy?" (or whatever attribute you judge about others). It is much easier to see someone else's 'stuff' than it is to see our own.

It is also a good idea to start with easy scenarios. Find some judgements that you see yourself saying all the time. It might be something like, "Those people are so stupid" and you notice yourself saying that often. "How could they be so stupid?" This would be a good place to start.

The reason that someone being stupid bothers you is that somewhere you have received the message that you are stupid. For someone who does not believe they are stupid, there is no reaction to someone else being stupid. They can just ignore it and walk away or they wouldn't have the thought in the first place. However, when we have shadow beliefs that we are also stupid, then it has more of a trigger for us. The reason the trigger is there is that we have a buried belief about it.

A sure-fire place to find our shadow self is in our opinions of our family. This is a treasure trove of belief patterns that are deeply ingrained because we lived with them for so long. Our parents, siblings and other relatives can easily trigger our childhood issues. Search for thoughts you have maybe of a parent that you also see in yourself. As much as we hate to admit it, we often repeat what our parents did even though we swore we would not be like them!

Or choose another family member, like a sibling. You can be almost certain that any judgement you have of a sibling is a shadow side of yourself. I have seen this many times in my work. I remember one day sitting with my friend Ernie who helped me with so much of my clearing work.

We were having lunch together and I was sharing something about my sister's life experience and he grinned and said, "And does that sound like you?" I was taken aback. I had no idea that the foundation of what I had just explained was exactly what I was experiencing in my life.

It appeared to be completely different because she lives her life differently than I do. What Ernie helped me realize is that underneath it I was acting from the same childhood belief that my sister was. And if I was judging it in her then the truth was that I was judging that part of myself. As I said, it can be hard to see for ourselves what is lurking underneath our thoughts.

Because we have been living from our basic thoughts and beliefs for so long, they are as natural as breathing. It really helps to have someone else on board to help us identify what we are digging for. This is particularly true for the judgments we have. It can be downright painful to look at them in some situations, but the rewards are well worth the risk of being honest with ourselves.

Once we are willing and prepared to truly see our judgments as the mirror for what we don't like about ourselves, we have the greatest tool for release. I will share specific tools and activities in the next chapter to help you identify your barriers to the real you – the beautiful, abundant, joyous you.

Another way to *find it* is to look at the people who can push your buttons. You know who they are. They know just what to say to get you going and sometimes all it takes is a certain look or a word or two. What is that trigger? Why does it have such power over you? What do you hate about it? To use the 'stupid' example, I have a friend who told me his mother can push his buttons and all it takes is a look.

So, in writing this, I called him and asked for more details. He said that she just gives him this 'you're stupid' look. I think we've all been on the receiving end of a look like that at one point in our lives. The reality is, if he didn't believe he was stupid or be fearful about being stupid, that look would have no charge for him. I've had many challenges in my own life, but being stupid is not one of them.

So, if someone gave me that look, I would simply ask what that look is about or ignore it. There would not be an emotional charge so I wouldn't read the look the same way. Again, our responses come from our beliefs. If we believe we are stupid, we will read the look as 'you're stupid!' and it will be irritating.

Another way to find our unsupporting beliefs is to look at patterns in our lives. Do you see similar circumstances repeating over and over? Money is always a good example for this one. I did some clearing work with someone I know recently. We'll call her Amy. Here's the story.

First the motor died in her daughter's car. Her daughter, let's call her Bee, couldn't afford to fix it but needed a car to get to work. Amy found a used motor for $500 and fortunately Bee found someone who said he could put it in the car for free. So Amy, after having the car towed once, paid to have it towed again to the man's house who was going to put the motor in.

It turned out this fellow didn't have the equipment to install the motor so the car had to be towed again to another garage where the motor was finally hooked up after a new motor and three towing bills! A couple of weeks before this Amy's dog injured himself and needed $1800 surgery.

Then, after fixing Bee's car, Amy's car needed repairs. I think you're getting the picture. I finally said to Amy that there might be some underlying beliefs about money and we did some clearing. When I asked a while later how things were going, she didn't really think about it again. But, I haven't heard of any major money grabbers since.

That is what I mean about a pattern. It can also show up in all aspects of our life. One common one is in relationships. Sometimes people date the same person over and over just wearing a different body suit. Some people are always dating people that aren't really available.

Maybe the other person is married or lives far away or works away. Every person they date is different but the pattern is the same. There is an underlying belief that is attracting someone who is unavailable. My thought would be that it would be around not believing that you deserve to have someone in your life or a fear of commitment.

By looking at such patterns we can get an idea of where we are being influenced by a subconscious belief. Those beliefs will keep impacting us in the same way until we do the work to discover what it is and release it.

There is another important tool of discovery and that is our self talk. Are you kind to yourself with your thoughts or are you your worst critic? Pay attention to your self-talk to bring some awareness to it. Most often our critical thoughts run through our minds without us really noticing what they are.

Once you make the decision to be conscious of your thoughts, you have taken the first step to change them. We can't change the program if we are not even aware of what our self-talk is. It takes awareness to change our program from self-judgement to being kind to ourselves. Knowing what we are thinking is another way of seeing what needs to be cleared.

I have discussed a variety of ways that we can search for our shadow self. That is the first step. We have to find it before we can free it. In the next chapter I will offer the tools to help not only become aware of our shadow self but to then clear the hidden beliefs that we discover are holding us back.

Peace Will Come

Do not doubt that peace will come.
When you see nations at war, hold onto your
faith in the Light
The final energies of fear will play themselves
out
and in their place Love will reign.
Stand strong in the face of fear
and claim, "I believe in Love.
The world rejoices in Light."

Chapter Six - Tools for Release

The fundamental key to releasing limiting beliefs and thoughts is awareness. Once we intentionally begin to monitor our thoughts and look for hidden beliefs, we are living in awareness and our lives can improve. Without this intention, we remain on the wheel, spinning through life and being bounced around as if it was some outside force that was creating our experiences.

That is simply not the case. We are the creators of our experience, either consciously or unconsciously. My goal in this book is to support you in bringing that truth into your conscious experience. What I am offering in this chapter is a variety of tools - methods of discovery – that will help you step off the wheel and move into awareness.

I would recommend buying a nice journal to record your activities from this chapter. It will allow you to have all your insights in one place and also to check back at a later date and see for yourself just how much has changed. Let's quickly review why you would want to be doing this work.

Our subconscious, limiting beliefs sabotage our lives without us even being aware. They keep us from fulfilling our dreams. They cause us to give up on believing that life could be anything different than what it is. They lead us into accepting a small life instead of living large. They steer us away from change and they cause us to repeat the patterns of yesterday.

Limiting beliefs have a huge impact on our lives and not for the betterment of our life conditions! If you are not convinced by now that it is important to do this work, you will be after you begin to discover and release some of the beliefs that are holding you back. Now let's move on to the first activity or tool to *find* what you want to *free*.

Every time we have a strong feeling that we do not acknowledge or express, it becomes trapped within the body. We all have a vital life force that runs through the body. It is the difference between life and death. When a person dies, the life force leaves the body and the breathing stops.

Therefore, this life force is our vitality. The more free flowing it is, the healthier we are. What many people don't know is that, when we stuff our feelings inside, we are storing them in the body. What happens when we do this is that the life force then cannot flow as freely. It creates road blocks that stop the life force from running through the channel that it was on.

The more we stuff our true feelings, the more road blocks we build. Eventually the body begins to slow down, deprived of the vital energy that keeps it youthful and healthy. This can show up in the body as aches and pains, arthritis or other ailments. Any physical symptom, according to my beliefs and experience, is an opportunity to see what is being stored in the body that does not belong in the body – as in emotions!

Our bodies are sensory machines. We have physical senses like touch, hearing and taste - and emotional responses, like love, sorrow, and happiness. There is a difference between feelings and emotions. Feelings are body sensations and emotions involve the thinking mind.

I might feel butterflies in my stomach when my new love holds my hand. That physical feeling can appear before I make the conscious connection to the emotion of love. Once we add emotions to the feelings they intensify. This intensity can feel overwhelming, especially in today's society where many of us are not taught how to manage these feelings and emotions.

In the example of holding hands, it is a good feeling and the love is most often allowed to flow freely. However, in a situation where we feel threatened and the emotion is less charming, we often suppress what is coming forward instead of expressing it.

An example would be living with someone who is aggressive. Because of their nature, it may not feel safe to express our true feelings when they cause us to feel anger or fear. When we feel it but don't express it, those emotions become stored in the body and restrict our vitality. And where are they stored? They are held within our cells as memories.

Every time we come into a similar situation we relate to the memory of that fearful or uncomfortable event and we respond by contracting. There's no room in a contracted body for life force and joy. And, there's no space for a new response to come forward.

The cells are full of fearful thoughts and constricted. That is why it's so important to use these tools and start living in awareness. They will help you stay in the moment. Awareness allows you to manage the day-to-day constriction.

Becoming aware of your thoughts is a great gift to yourself. Our minds, when left unmanaged, tend to focus on the negative and get lost in worry and concern. Our thoughts do create, so it is important to get a grip on our thinking. When we are aware of our thoughts then we can turn them around into something positive and focus on what we would like to have in our lives, not everything we don't want.

If eighty percent of your thoughts are about worry or self-blame or judgement, then the twenty percent of positive thoughts aren't going to have much impact on the overall state of your life. Plus, allowing the mind to spin and be negative all the time leads to more stress and illness. That is why the first tool I am going to share with you is to support you in becoming aware of your thoughts in every moment.

A few years ago I was creeping through rush hour traffic on my way to work when a car suddenly turned out of its lane and ran into me! The interesting thing is, I knew exactly what I was thinking when it happened. My thought, just before the accident was, "If I get that job in Windsor I'm going to need a new car."

I think this remarkable for two reasons. One, I knew what I was thinking at that very moment which I was proud of because it shows me my thoughts are being managed. Secondly, the universe promptly responded to my request and provided me with a newer car as my old one was a write-off from the accident!

That story clearly shows that, one, our thoughts create and two, the universe provides. Again, it doesn't always look like we think it will, but when we are willing to see that we got what we asked for, it is really quite fun to watch it all unfolding! This is an example to show the benefits of managing our thoughts. The more we make the connection between our thoughts and what happens in our external world, the easier it is to change. Being mindful – that is being in awareness as we walk this life – is a great skill and leads to peace of mind and all around well-being.

The *Outside Eyes* Tool

Here is the first tool that I want you to use if you have a busy mind (or if you just want to be more in the moment – living in the now). Do not dismiss the simplicity of what is offered here. It is said that the truth is simple and I believe it. It is our ego mind that wants to complicate things and make them seem more important somehow.

This tool is very effective in keeping us in the moment. It is simply to be aware of the natural world around you. That's why I call it the *Outside Eyes Tool.* You cannot be noticing the beautiful poppies growing on the side of the road and spinning in your head at the same time. Being in nature can pull you into the wonder of the moment if you pay attention and really choose to see what is around you.

Just being outdoors helps people feel better. I believe much of our misery in these times comes from our disconnection to the natural world. Being in nature and appreciating the beauty that it provides usually means being happier. If you're not a nature lover, notice the architecture around you. Where is the light reflecting? What are the colours around you and the shapes?

Get out of your head and really see with your eyes. This is like a walking meditation. Instead of walking around with a busy mind, walk in the state of being very present with what is around you. Be aware of every step you take. This way you begin to still the mind and when thoughts to come you have a much better chance of noticing them and being conscious of your own internal dialogue.

Of course, like all the tools I will offer here, it will not work if you don't try it. Make a note in your journal to go for a walk at some point in your day and really notice your surroundings. Then, after your walk, just check in to see how you feel compared to when you started your walk.

In reality, there are very few moments in our lives that are difficult. It is where we allow our minds to go that creates our worries. Stay present in this moment and you will have more moments with no worry. That is a good beginning to noticing what is positive in your life and choosing empowering thoughts.

The *Ten Times* Tool

The next tool that I would like to share with you is a simple method of releasing feelings and emotions at the time that they occur. This tool doesn't necessarily dig into the subconscious to retrieve the hidden beliefs, but it allows us to release in the moment so that we are not adding to the storage box in the subconscious. Again, there is great power in simplicity. Make a commitment to try it so that you can see how effective it is.

Here it is: the next time you are feeling an emotion - be it anger, discouragement, disappointment, resentment - repeat to yourself ten times what it is you are feeling. For example, you might say, "I am feeling *so* disappointed. I am *feeling* so disappointed. I am feeling so *disappointed*"..... and on until you have repeated the same statement at least ten times.

By the time I get to the sixth or seven statement a big sigh comes out of me. I still repeat all ten but I can feel it leaving my body right away. This is key. If we do this every time we have a feeling that we can't fully express or discuss with someone, releasing it in this way will keep it from anchoring in the body.

It is important to do this as soon as the feeling appears. Otherwise, if you don't acknowledge it, it will become anchored in the body and affirm the subconscious belief that it stemmed from.

As I said, this tool is not getting to hidden beliefs but it is keeping the body clearer of stored emotions and therefore allowing more life force to flow through you. When you do the clearing work, you want to be sure that you aren't bringing new experiences into the body that are unhealthy and unsupportive to your quest for a joyful life. So be sure to try this tool the next time something stirs for you emotionally.

The *Pranic Breath* Tool

The *Pranic Breath* Tool is another method of releasing from the body. There is a column that runs through the center of our bodies where the prana, or life force energy flows. It runs from the perineum (between the anus and the genitals) all the way up through the body and out the crown of the head. We can use this column to disperse intense emotions throughout the body, with the breath as the guide.

Use this tool to release strong emotions when you are feeling overwhelmed. Learning to use the breath is powerful for so many reasons. We cannot be anxious and breathing deeply at the same time. Deep, intentional breath equals calm. In today's world, it is a tool that is too often overlooked in managing our feelings and state of well-being.

Right now, as you are reading this, sit with your back straight and legs uncrossed and take seven breaths in through the nose and out through the mouth with a sigh. Pay attention to your body as you do this and see how you feel. For women this is a simple way to release adrenalin from the body.

Adrenalin is beneficial for men but not for women. Females become stressed with too much adrenalin in their bodies whereas men benefit from it. However, using the breath to manage our emotions is effective for everyone and a simple but powerful tool to keep the life force flowing through our bodies. Use *The Pranic Breath Tool* when you are feeling overwhelmed by emotion or any uncomfortable state of being.

To start, join your thumb and middle finger to see the size of your pranic tube that runs through the center of the body. Imagine that tube and, as you breathe in, imagine pulling life force energy up from the earth into your tube and down from the sky into your tube at the same time.

Imagine the energy coming up from the earth and down from the sky and meeting at your heart. On the out breath, send that energy out from that central pranic tube to your entire body. So, as you breathe out, imagine that the emotional energy you are feeling is being dispersed throughout your entire body via the pranic tube.

It is like a long, tubular fluorescent light bulb. The light disperses through the entire tube. That is how you envision the emotional energy dispersing throughout the body. This allows your emotions to move through the body instead of lodging in one place. It also keeps the energy of the emotions flowing so that they do not become too much to handle.

Just practicing this type of breathing once a day will keep you healthier. It keeps you balanced between heaven and earth, so to speak, and will help to open the channels that are blocked because of stuck feelings or emotions that have been lodged in a certain area of the body.

The *Three Step Awareness* Tool

Another tool I use to recognize fears that arise I call the *Three Step Awareness Tool.* This one is working through the ego's desire to keep us doing what we have always done instead of stepping into a new expression of ourselves. Whenever we feel resistance to doing something new, it is this ego stance that has a hold on us.

Or, maybe it is not even something new that we are contemplating but something that we have to do where we have an association with a negative outcome. When I first planned a recent trip I was excited because things were synchronistically falling into place. I had learned during a meditation that I was to go to Toronto and offer my sound workshop there.

I also got that I was to go the following month. I contacted the only person I know in Toronto and it turned out that he was driving up on the 5th of the following month and offered me a drive! This is when I know I am on the right track. I was feeling excited. However, the body was bringing up a familiar response of resistance. I wasn't quite sure what it was and didn't pursue it at the time. So, it showed up the next day as resistance.

This is where the *Three Step Awareness Tool* comes in. Very often when we are moving toward something new or something with a negative historical association, the ego wants to protect us by saying, "Don't do that!" This is what I was feeling after the initial excitement. When you feel resistance and you have done clearing work around the resistance, you know that this tool is required.

If you feel excited about what you are considering doing but then fear comes up, it is time to be aware that ego is trying to keep you from growing into the accomplishment that your soul desires. The trick is to feel the fear and do it anyway. If not, the fear wins. And when our lives are ruled by fear, it's not much fun.

To walk through the fear is like a test from our soul to see if we are truly ready for the next leap in our evolution. When we feel the fear and push it to the side and do what we were initially excited about, the ego learns that it is safe this time to do this activity and, by the action of doing, we have created a new memory pathway that is no longer bringing up fear.

The *Three Step Awareness* recognizes the three stages of moving into something new: *excitement, resistance, and success*. Excitement is the initial inspiration that led you to choose the new event or action. Resistance is the fear response that the ego sends out when you are stepping out of your comfort zone. Success comes after you decide to walk through the fear and take the action required to fulfill your inspiration and realize success.

The resistance that the ego presents is a common occurrence whenever we are stepping out of our comfort zone. And yet, if we never step out of our comfort zone our lives will never change. If you are happy with your life then this is not a problem. However, if you are choosing a more exciting and prosperous and loving life, then you will need to take that step and walk through the fear into your joy.

Just having the awareness of how this happens allows you to have the wisdom to tell your ego fears to step aside and march right out of your comfort zone and into the new experience that you are choosing to have in your life.

That is what I did for my trip to Toronto and I was beautifully supported on that trip. My hosts were most gracious, I received healing from people I had just met, and offered successful workshops. Now, the next time I plan to travel, my ego can relate to this joyful experience instead of the more challenging experiences of the past.

At this point you may be wondering, what if I walk through the fear and have another negative experience just like the last one? In that case, you have some clearing work to do around the experience and what your hidden beliefs are bringing to you regarding your unconscious expectations. What were the challenges that were there? The answer to that question will lead you to your hidden beliefs that need to be cleared so you can choose a different experience next time.

The *Reverse View Mirror* Tool

The greatest tool in discovering our hidden beliefs is the one that requires courage and a willingness to be vulnerable but it's worth it! The *Reverse View Mirror* takes us to those shadows that I have been talking about. Because our shadow side can be elusive, I recommend doing this activity with a friend, although it is not necessary.

In order to release our limiting beliefs we first have to find them. Sometimes having a friend or two with us when doing the *Reverse View Mirror* can help us recognize personal attributes that we might be inclined to deny about ourselves. What you are finding in this activity is truly what you don't like about yourself.

In order to live the life of our dreams, we must be coming from a place of self-love. Otherwise, we create our experience based on lack of love and wonder why we are not happy. The benefit of doing all this clearing work is that we release the aspects of ourselves that we don't like which then lead to more loving experiences in our lives.

Remember this as you courageously step into the shadows to find the pieces of you that are lurking there. The more you find and release, the more you really start to truly love yourself and start creating the life you have yearned for.

It's time to get out your journal and write down all the people in your life that you don't like. Just make a list of everyone you can think of who irritates you or pushes your buttons or whom you dislike. Your list might include co-workers, siblings, friends, your partner, a neighbor or even one of your children. Take time to write your list of people before reading further.

Next I would like you to take maybe three people on your list and write down what it is you don't like about them. You can get to the others on your list later. Be honest with yourself. No filters. Everything about them that irritates you or angers you or whatever it is, list those attributes. Do this now before reading on.

Great. You have your list of characteristics that you don't like about people in your life. Now comes the interesting part. For each irritating characteristic that you have written down, I want you to ask yourself where you have that same characteristic within yourself.

If you wrote that Suzie is disrespectful and never acknowledges you, where do you not acknowledge yourself? Where are you disrespectful to yourself? Not necessarily to others but to yourself! As I have said, everything in your life experience is about you.

So, even if you can recognize where you are disrespectful to others at times, the truth is that ultimately you are disrespectful to yourself. That is the *Reverse View Mirror*. What you see with your eyes in your external environment is what you believe about yourself in your internal environment.

Before I was released from my job, my workplace provided plenty of opportunities to use the reverse view mirror! One of the biggest issues I had with my coworkers was gossip. I hate gossip! It is destructive and I am so sensitive that I always know when people are talking about me behind my back.

And yet, when I looked honestly at my behavior, there were times when I would talk about someone who was not present for the conversation. I found I was pulled into this mostly with family. Once I was aware of this, I clearly stated that I was not willing to engage.

Looking deeper, I had to ask myself where I spoke ill of myself. This is the part of turning all the way around to not just how we are with others regarding the attribute that we are exploring but how we are with ourselves with that attribute. Now I had the full picture.

I was feeling like I wasn't doing a very good job in my new position, and I was self-critical. How that showed up in my external world was to have co-workers who were critical of me – showing me my own self-criticism.

Explore this for yourself. Take the attributes that you identified on your list and put them in the mirror so-to-speak. Look to see where you believe those things about yourself. This step is the beginning of releasing.

Once we bring awareness to something it cannot exist in the same way that it did. We can no longer pretend that it is not there because we know it is there. Once you stop believing in Santa Claus, if you ever did, he is never as real as he was, even if you want to keep the illusion alive.

I know this piece can be hard to grasp so let me give you another example of how it works. Today I was working with someone whose daughter-in-law had sent her an email earlier in the day, asking that she and her husband not visit in the evenings. This person is a new grandmother and, like most grandmothers, adores the baby.

Being told that she couldn't visit in the evenings felt quite painful. Like most people, she wanted to blame her daughter-in-law for setting up those parameters and not including them in the 'family' decision around when to visit.

That's not how it works. It was not about the daughter-in-law but about the person I was working with. Every experience comes from our inner beliefs! So, we explored what her daughter-in-law was showing her. It appeared that her daughter was attempting to control her life.

Where was my client a controlling person? Where did she need to be in control in her own life? It felt like she was being kept away from the baby. Where did she keep herself away from things that she cared about? I felt that perhaps her daughter was just setting clear boundaries, but she couldn't see that, so we explored where she did not have clear boundaries.

By the end of our conversation, with some clearing work, my client felt much better about the email and was able to respond from a place of clarity, without the emotional pain she was feeling when we started our session. And the beauty is that, having cleared those beliefs, her daughter-in-law may well disregard the request for no night-time visits. Because my client no longer needs to be shown the belief system (the internal) that was cleared, the external experience can change.

This is the most valuable tool that I have given you in this book. If you are serious about finding your way out of the prison of your subconscious beliefs, then you will be using this tool for years to come. Once your shadows have been revealed, use the other tools offered here to start releasing them.

A lot of this you can do on your own. However, if you are in a position to do so, I would strongly recommend using other methods that clear the limiting beliefs from your subconscious. The reason is that the modalities I mentioned previously, like Access Consciousness or my Release Technique, or Emotional Freedom Technique immediately release the belief that has surfaced and clears it from your memory. There are many layers to each belief, so aspects of it will continue to surface.

It is because some of the stones you placed on your wall of protection were related to the same initial experience. You kept adding to the protection that you felt you needed to reinforce the wall. You may take one stone off but there will be more as you dig deeper. As I have said, you can search out a practitioner of Theta Healing, Access Consciousness, or visit my website www.rashana.ca to book a Freedom Release Technique session with me or join my ongoing group clearing calls. Find a healing modality that releases from the subconscious as the above techniques do.

Congratulations on making it this far. You have done a lot of work already. The more you realize about the hidden self, the happier you become. You will no longer think "I should be happy. I have this and this and this and yet there is something missing". Now you have tools to find what that something is. Continue to use the tools provided and walk with the determination to be aware of all that is holding you back. The next step is to be sure to honour your achievements and keep your life balanced between searching for the limitations and celebrating the releases. Balance is always key to a joyous and happy life.

Wisdom

Wise is the heart that awakens in the morning
rejoicing the new day.
Wise is the heart that rises each day with well
wishes for one and all.
Wise is the Soul who resides in the Light.
Cast away your fears Dear Ones. They
serve you not.
Lift your thoughts above the dense patterns
of pain and despair to see the Light that
shines above the clouds.
Your eyes will follow your mind.
With thoughts of darkness you see fear and
hardship.
With thoughts of light you see opportunity
and hope.
Choose wisely Dear Ones.
For more than ever, each thought is a
creation.

Chapter Seven - Why it Takes Courage to Become Rich

Have you ever heard of people who win millions in the lottery and a year or two later they're just as poor as they were before they had their lucky break? Why do you think that is? Most of us believe we would be so happy if we won the big one. If I only had money all my worries would be over. I would be happy at last.

And yet, this is often not the case. If we have beliefs of lack and limitation we will not likely allow ourselves to stay rich or even become rich in the first place. But it goes deeper than that. It's important to take a good look at what it would mean to be rich, in all aspects of our lives.

Many people dream of being rich, but when you are really determined to become abundant and turn your life around, there is a lot to consider. How will your relationships with your friends change? If you want to go out to dinner at a nice restaurant, will your friends be able to afford it?

You could offer to pay but how would they feel if you were always buying so that they could come along? After a while they may feel inadequate in comparison to you and find reasons why they can't join you. Would you come to resent them over time because you always had to pay? Do you think your friendships would have to change if you become more successful?

What about family? Would family members judge you if you were to buy a big house or travel all the time? Would they say you had changed or think of you as a snob because you could do things they could not? Let's face it, if you grew up with beliefs of lack, your family no doubt contributed to it.

So if family members have attitudes around money such as rich people are selfish or mean because they think only of themselves, what will your family think of you once you are rich? Most people do not live the same way in abundance as they do in lack.

It's important to give this some thought and explore how you think things in your life would change if you found yourself living without any financial concerns what-so-ever. Would family members resent your success? Would they resent your big house or nice new car? Would they judge you as being a show-off now that you are so rich?

Are there family members who wouldn't understand your decisions? Suddenly you may find that every relative that you never knew you had is at your doorstep hoping for a handout. How do you say no when they know you have lots of money? How would it feel to be judged by your family?

What I am talking about are not certain outcomes but they are probable outcomes and worth considering. Without exploring these aspects of abundance honestly, the thoughts of losing friends or loved ones could keep you from stepping into the riches that you think you desire. They could be holding you back from choosing wealth without your conscious awareness. It's best to look at these things now and get them settled in your mind so that they won't stop you when the time comes to step into your abundance.

Having wealth and prosperity also comes with responsibility. What a great problem it is to have to worry about where to invest your money so you don't have to pay so many taxes! At least it sounds like a great problem, but some people get so tied up in it that it takes the joy out of being rich.

And who is going to look after the big house with all the fancy gadgets and technology when you travel? The more possessions you have the more worries you have. I knew a woman who worked in Mexico as a teacher for a year. One of the parents told her that she worried about the safety of her children every day because they were so rich.

Life can be easier but maybe not as simple when you're rich. It can mean being a target in many ways. How would you handle that? Would you move to a bigger community where no one knows you? Would you move to a gated community? Would you be happy living that way?

Why do I say it takes courage to be rich? It is because you have to change who you were and become somebody new. You could not be rich and be who you were if who you were lived in lack. Something would have to change. If you must change then you will be showing up in the world differently.

People you have known for years may look at you and say, "You've changed." And it would be true, but how would it feel for you to have people say that. Maybe they would feel like they couldn't relate to you anymore. Is that OK? If you lost old friends, who would your new friends be?

I know I have little tolerance for prestige. I don't believe anyone is better than another person simply because of income or social status. So having money for me does not mean stepping up the social ladder. That means I have to find friends who are down to earth but who can have the same liberties in life that money affords.

This doesn't apply to every situation in life. If you are someone who is happy to be at home most of the time and have people over for dinner, then the changes may not impact you as much. However, for people who have been waiting for more adventure in life and the freedom that money brings in that regard, then you may realize that friendships will change.

One of the biggest steps in all of this work is allowing ourselves to become someone new. We have been who we were for as long as we have been on this earth. When we decide to do the clearing work that releases our limiting beliefs then we must allow ourselves to change the person who no longer holds those beliefs.

This can be scary at times because it means so much in our lives has to shift. When we think differently, what shows up in our lives becomes different. Of course this all leads to forward growth and walking into the greatest expression of our full potential. It's just that you can't be your full potential and pretend to be small.

Many people hold themselves back so that they won't outshine those around them. This serves no one. When we stand tall and shine brightly, we are giving others permission to do the same. When we step into abundance and improve all aspects of our lives, we are giving others the invitation to grow and expand as well.

Some will want to follow and others will believe that it is impossible or too much work and they will stay in the shadows of their beliefs. The choice belongs to the individual and there is no judgement around what each person chooses. The point is to understand that this work will bring about change in all aspects of your life.

The more prepared you are in your mind, the more you will allow it to flow. And life will show you where your beliefs are holding you back. The more you do this work, the more you come to recognize when there is a limiting belief that is surfacing, wanting to keep you from moving forward.

That is a wonderful opportunity to muster up your courage to face another shadow, do more clearing work and walk through the fear. It is an opportunity because, on the other side, is success. Every time you release something you are getting closer to the truth of you – the fullness of your soul expression on this earth. As you do, life just keeps improving!

I believe this journey of healing and releasing is a life-long one. As long as we are living in this world, things will come up to challenge us or cause us to explore the inner self. If you think you have done all your work, congratulations. It's great to recognize your accomplishments. Just don't be surprised when life offers up a new challenge or feeling that is uncomfortable.

That is what this human expression is all about. The contrast keeps the journey exciting. And once you step onto this road of personal growth there is no going back. I remember times when I would wish that I could just pretend that I wasn't 'aware' so that I could walk in the bliss of ignorance.

But, once you know that more is possible, it is impossible to pretend it is not. Those moments were just fleeting desires for life to be easy. What they were truly reflecting was that I was still carrying beliefs that weren't supporting the ease of the journey that I now know is possible.

I have included this chapter to bring to your awareness the possible ways that your life will change as you grow into your true self. Look at all aspects of your life and consider how they may change. This would include relationships with family, friends, coworkers, etc.

Also look at factors such as where life would lead you if you were living your dreams – who you would be with, where you would live, what you would be doing? Then ask yourself how much you are willing to change to bring all of that into reality.

It may not feel like it takes courage to make these changes, but when faced with friendships fading or family members not understanding you, the reality of it touches your soul in ways that you may not have anticipated.

A Prayer

May the Love of the Divine flow through me.
May it fill my every thought with purity and
hope.
May it ring on every word like a blessing.
May it emanate from my heart
like a mother's love;
so that all my expressions are filling the world
with joy, encouragement and grace.

Chapter Eight - Tools to Celebrate Success

Now that you have cleared many beliefs and limitations that your subconscious has been holding onto, it is time to embrace the new you and celebrate what you have accomplished.

When we do clearing we are creating space for something new. It is important to consciously embrace that newness and to fill the space with empowering beliefs. The reason for this journey is to become the fullness of our soul's expression.

If we don't consciously embrace new, powerful beliefs about ourselves, we could easily slip back into the old patterns of thought. It is important to use these tools for success to impress upon your subconscious that you are not the same person you used to be.

If you accomplish something in your life and don't celebrate it, the subconscious will not register the success and will want to repeat the old pattern again and again. Once you affirm your forward progress and make a strong reference mentally of your accomplishment, the subconscious will move onto the next task.

Exploring Your Core Values

If we stumble through life without direction we are usually running away from what we do not want instead of walking toward what we desire. Knowing what you value in life can help set clear boundaries and keep you on course to success. This tool is an exploration of your *Core Values*.

We all have values that we live by but again, often they are at an unconscious level. By bringing our values into our awareness, we can set clear limits on what we are willing to do or not and also who we are willing to have in our lives or not.

It is much easier to have a clear direction when we know, for example, that this person fits into our life because their values resonate with ours, or you're not willing to work for company X because they do not. When we are strongly aware of our bottom line, it is easier to keep going in the right direction and not get distracted away from our truth.

To do the *Core Values Tool*, get your journal and write down what you believe to be the values that are most important to you. Just list whatever comes to mind. Make a list of at least ten. After you have made your list you could do an online search of values to get a broader perspective of some values that may not have come to mind for you. You can have as many as you wish for the first step of this exercise.

Once you have your list, choose the top ten values that are the most important to you. It is important to identify the ones that you know mean the most to you. Now, put your top ten in order with number one being the absolute most important value and number ten being the least important of the ten.

There is a reason for doing this. Often what we first think of as the most important changes as we narrow the list. If you do all of this activity you have the opportunity to discover this, so complete the top ten priority list. Then, the last step is to pick the top three.

Again, your list may change. The top three in your list of ten may not end up being the absolute three most important values to you. The reason for doing this activity so thoroughly is that, when you have your top three, you can remember what they are and be aware, in every decision you make, whether you are honouring your core values.

The more you make decisions based on your own truth instead of what someone else may project onto you, the clearer you become in your life's journey and the more you learn that you can trust yourself. If you can trust yourself to make clear decisions, then you can trust yourself to be successful and abundant.

When you make decisions that are out of harmony with your core self, you learn that you are not trustworthy and it impacts every aspect of your daily existence. When you don't trust yourself, how do you think it impacts your thoughts of others? Knowing that everything in your experience comes from your thoughts and beliefs, it means that you don't trust others either. The lack of trust is reflected in your life experience.

Getting back to values, when you know your top three values and make your decisions to honour those values, you live in integrity with your true self and it is a powerful way of being in the world. So, complete this activity as outlined and keep your list handy!

Seeing Is Believing - Or Believe It and You Will See It

The second tool I would like to share I call, *Seeing is Believing*, although the opposite is really the truth. In reality, believing is seeing. That is, what we believe we see. However, for this tool, I am asking you to see what you are looking for.

To start with I would like you to get your journal and put these headings across a double page: home, family, partner, friends, work, play. In point form under each heading, write down what you desire life to offer in each category. Don't just consider physical or environmental factors, take it a step deeper into the values that you have already identified as important to you.

For example, under the 'home' heading, you might put things such as 3 bedrooms, sunny with lots of windows and in the country. But you may also want to add, cozy, a sanctuary, quiet or a safe space for your children, comfortable with friendly neighbours. The values can end up being more important than the more tangible aspects of your list, so be sure to include them. Think of your top three values and how they would relate to each heading.

Once you have your list, take some time to think about where those things already exist in your life. For example, when I was dreaming of owning a house, I discovered that someone was building a new house on a little street that I like to walk down. It is a dead end street, so it is quiet, with a world class view. I would pretend that it was my house. As it developed I was very happy with the choice of windows and the siding.

By noticing that there was this beautiful house in my world, I was bringing my own house closer to my experience. Or, being single, I was also feeling like I was ready to open up to a loving partner in my life. By noticing other couples and people meeting their new lovers, I was celebrating with them and recognizing that romantic love already existed in my life experience.

In that way, I was seeing that love does exist in my world already and new love was coming into my experience. What we focus on is what we magnetize into our lives. By looking for what we desire to have in our lives we bring it ever closer.

We see what we look for. It is like buying a new red car and all of a sudden you notice red cars everywhere. It is because your focus is on your new red car and therefore you notice them in your experience. The same is true for your desires. Instead of focusing on what you don't have in relation to your wishes, look for where it already exists in your life.

If you find yourself feeling resentment for others who have what you want, it is time to do more clearing work. By holding resentment you will be pushing what you are asking for away from you. Your resentment will give you more to be resentful about because you will create what you are focused on.

By doing the opposite and choosing to see that your desires already exist around you, you will be bringing them closer and closer with every thought. The more you clear through this, the closer you are to having what you desire. If you hold on to resentment, you are really just harming yourself. You are the one who stands to benefit from the clearing work.

The following poem speaks beautifully to what our souls are yearning for. Our soul – the deepest aspect of our being – wants to be living a glorious life. That is why we are always desiring more. Many of you may have read this verse before. It was attributed to Nelson Mandela but it was written by Marianne Williamson. It speaks so beautifully about the importance of stepping into our fullness and celebrating all that we are. Here it is:

Born to Manifest the Glory

"Our deepest fear is not that we are inadequate.
Our deepest fear is that we are powerful beyond measure.
It is our light, not our darkness, that most frightens us.
We ask ourselves, who am I to be brilliant, gorgeous,
talented, and fabulous?
Actually, who are you not to be?
You are a child of God.
Your playing small doesn't serve the world.
There's nothing enlightened about shrinking so
that other people won't feel insecure around you.
We are all meant to shine, as children do.

We are born to make manifest the glory of God that is within us.
It's not just in some of us, it's in everyone.
And as we let our own light shine,
we unconsciously give other
people permission to do the same.
As we are liberated from our own fear,
our presence automatically liberates others."

by Marianne Williamson

If God does not fit into your belief system, substitute that word with 'love'. In my understanding it is one and the same. What I like about that poem is that she expresses so beautifully the great need for us all to be walking in our full, radiant self, shining proudly all that we are out to the world.

That doesn't mean we go around bragging about ourselves all the time or being boastful in any way. It just means that we speak with confidence and we stand tall, feeling our worthiness in the world. When we truly recognize that within ourselves, we see it in others.

Be It

This leads me to another tool: *Be It*. We have learned that in order to be who we truly are, we have to know who we are not. That is what the first half of this book was about. As we clear the outdated, limiting beliefs, we are releasing who we are not.

By that I mean that we are not necessarily the people that society and our environment tell us we are. The pure, innocent and loving souls that are born into this world often get lost in childhood as we learn to cope in this world. To use this tool we have to do a little more exploring about where our beliefs about ourselves came from.

Every family seems to have labels for their children. You might be the serious, older child or the clown that entertains everyone or the less responsible and spoiled youngest child. These labels are just the beginning. Then we start school and our teachers define us as being a good student or a bad student, restless or intelligent.

Then classmates and our peers do the same. We move into the teenage years and try on a few different personalities or get stuck in one that works and we carry that into adulthood. All these different roles are our way of fitting in to our families and the greater world. They may not reflect the truth of who we are at all. They are created so that we can survive by fitting into the family of humanity. Whatever works is what we adopt as our personality.

Now, in this process of discovering who we *really* are, we first need to identify the roles we took on in our families and with our friends and coworkers. I was always shy, quiet and withdrawn. I didn't want to be seen in the world. As a result, some people thought I was a snob because I was too shy to talk to anyone.

I'm sure I was outwardly labeled as shy many times by my mother. I cringe now when I see parents speaking in front of their children as being shy or aggressive. They will be whatever we want them to be in order to get our love. (Not that I blame my mother for this. She was doing the best she could as a parent, just as all parents do.)

Others thought I was a good girl because I wouldn't do anything to rock the boat. Underneath was this great desire for excitement and creativity with no outlet or form of expression because I was too timid to even let out a squeak. There were many other factors that impacted this, but you get the idea. Who I appeared to be on the outside was a very dimmed down version of my true self.

Using this example to get you started, I would like you to get your journal again and record all the people who influenced you growing up and who placed labels on you. What were those labels? What roles did you take on in order to fit into the world? What aspects of 'not you' are you ready to release? What truth of you is hiding in the shadows, ready to come to light? Take some time now to list the beliefs about you that came from parents, siblings, relatives, community members, teachers, friends and so on. Just ask yourself what people expected you to be in all those roles. Once you have your list, look at where those attributes are less than supportive or not reflecting the truth of who you know yourself to be.

You can use that list to do some more exploring to discover what limiting beliefs you could clear from this discovery. From my example of being shy, I could clear beliefs of not being worthy to be seen in the world. It could be related to recognizing my value and worthiness to be here and be heard. Once you have completed that, it is time to discover who you really are.

One way to discover who you really are is to ask yourself if money were no object and you never had to work another day in your life, what would you do? Would you garden all day or would you paint or play with children or do book work? What are you passionate about?

If you can't identify any passion, asking what you would do with your days will help you discover that. If you were to do something meaningful in the world, what would that be? Answering that question is another way to discover the deepest aspect of you. Record what you come up with and make a list of all your redeeming qualities – the pieces of you that feel like the real you, not the you that others labeled you as.

Find out who you really are or would like to be. Another way to get to the heart of this is to look at qualities that you admire about others. Think of people you respect and ask what it is about them that you admire?

Is it their integrity in living, their lifestyle, their contribution to the world? In your most brilliant self, who are you? What are all your redeeming qualities? This is not the place to have false humility. If you are good at something be honest about it and recognize yourself. Others will never acknowledge your attributes if you are not clear on them yourself.

Continue exploring until you feel that you have a good sense of who you are in the deepest recesses of your heart where all is healed and your most precious self awaits. Once you have recorded these qualities I would like to you celebrate each and every one. Take a moment and shout out loud every quality that you admire about yourself.

Here's one of mine: "I am so creative that I am continually inspired to bring more and more divine brilliance into the world." As I say this, my hands are in the air and I am celebrating me. I am becoming the truth of me and celebrating the process. I am exclaiming to the universe who I am and in the process, my subconscious gets the message that this is the new me.

"Hooray. I love me. I love everything about me. I love the remembering of who I am and I love the moments when I forget." Have a party. You can invite only yourself or you can invite several friends or family and go through this whole process and celebrate together.

You could help your family and friends understand more fully who you are becoming, just as you are discovering that for yourself. The point is to celebrate the new you. Celebrate every time you release and clear something so that you acknowledge that you have just moved closer to the real you. The more you do this work the more you feel like celebrating because life continues to become more meaningful, lighter and more joyful. Yay. How does it get any better than that?

Peace Will Come

Do not doubt that peace will come.
When you see nations at war,
hold onto your faith in the Light.
The final energies of fear will play themselves
out
and in their place Love will reign.
Stand strong in the face of fear and claim,
"I believe in Love. The world rejoices in
Light."

Chapter Nine - Believe It and Be It!

Here we are at the final stage of the journey. This is not to say that the work is over. As I like to say, the work is done when we check out! All the stages continue to cycle as life goes on. However, it is important to get to this stage as we go through the clearing and releasing process.

Believe it and be it! It is time to live in the fullness of who we are becoming. All the work that is done in the beginning of this process, with the identification of our limiting beliefs, is to get to this stage. As I have said many times, what we believe, we are. So, we must believe in the new person that we are evolving into so that we can be it and see it in our life experience.

Allow yourself to respond differently in the world. Adopt and use the new aspects of you that you have embraced after releasing the limiting beliefs. An example of this is me allowing people to support me after turning people away all of my life.

If I had not been willing to allow this into my life experience, only two days after releasing the limiting belief, I would not have the wonderful business partnership I now have and the great business success that I am enjoying as a result of it. If I had held onto the old me who walked alone and felt uncomfortable with people I didn't know, then I would not have allowed this new experience, even though I had cleared the belief.

Once we shift a limiting belief, life circumstances can start changing immediately. It is important to be aware of this and to be noticing when things change. The more we notice something, the more it becomes our reality. By giving it our attention we create more of the same. This is the greatest joy in doing this work. It seems miraculous in the beginning, how things shift.

It is amazing that our minds are so connected to our lives. Did you know that people with multiple personality disorder can have one medically diagnosed illness in one personality and that illness not be present with a different personality?! I find that amazing. It clearly shows that it is the mind that is creating the life experience.

Just as our limiting beliefs were impacting our life experience before being cleared, our new thoughts will transform into new beliefs. Once we start to see new experiences show up it is easy to believe how effective this release work is. Then we begin to create new belief systems, based on our more loving thoughts. When we are creating from a place of loving ourselves, our lives will change dramatically.

What we create when we are down on ourselves and not believing that we deserve abundance is dramatically different from what we create when we have cleared those beliefs and allow love and joy and prosperity to flow into our lives. By noticing all the changes and being aware of our new responses to the world, we will add to the new beliefs that we deserve all that we desire.

It is then important to be the person that we have become. The more we integrate each step – each release – the easier it will be for us to accept that new aspect of ourselves. Don't be concerned if your work seems to be moving slowly. A Chinese proverb states: *Be not afraid of moving slowly; be afraid only of standing still.*

The important thing is to continue to allow yourself to be who you are becoming. The more you release the past, the more you step into the brilliance that you were born with. We all have it within. It got covered by societal expectations and restrictions. The more we become the truth of who we are as we release, the more deeply we connect with that brilliance and allow it to come forward.

With every release we come closer to it and also feel safer allowing it to shine in the world. When we are not believing in our worthiness, we don't allow that bright light that we are to shine out into the world. Every time you declare the new you and walk taller in the world, you are being more truthful to the full expression of your soul. It is beautiful to watch it unfold.

There is such joy and clarity when you are no longer doubting yourself and looking for worth outside of yourself. The more you be it, the more you truly believe that you are not who you were. Day after day you become more of the truth of you when you consciously notice what comes up as fear, release it and then allow yourself to be the person that you just became without that fear.

We can monitor how we are doing at this final step of the process by what we see in the world. Are things changing in your life experience? Are new opportunities coming your way, or new friendships, or greater feelings of contentment? These are indications that you are releasing the old and stepping into the new you. If you feel nothing in your life experience is changing, then it is best to spend more time exploring where the limiting beliefs are.

When you get to the stage of *believe it and be it*, you should be seeing changes happening in your life. They may not come falling out of the sky and hit you on the head. They may be subtle, but you should be noticing them. Notice and celebrate. Right now, I feel so good about feeling so good. Celebrate every feeling that is an improvement in your life. Every positive thought will lead to more.

If, at this point, you feel like not much has changed, get your journal and list all the areas of your life that you have worked with before. Use headings such as family, career, friendships, entertainment, etc. Then list what your life looks right now in each category. By doing this you will have a record to use as a comparison further down the road.

It is also an opportunity to see the areas that you would like to be working on right now. This tool can help you see where your life has improved and maybe you didn't give it much attention or it was so subtle that you didn't recognize it. When you see things on your list that have improved, celebrate.

Make a mental note of the improvements and love yourself for making that change. Then ask if you are responding in the world as someone who has made that change. Are you being the new you in that regard or still thinking of yourself as the former you? Be sure to walk into the new you as you transform through this process. Whatever has not changed then requires more exploration and clearing.

Because your beliefs create your reality, you will not have success with this process unless you believe it is possible. If you read this book but do not believe it can be so easy to clear away the past and move into abundance then it won't happen for you. If you believe something is impossible, then it is.

My hope is, at this point, that you have used the tools given here and are already experiencing releases that are leading to new experiences in your life. That is what creates the belief. You get to see it for yourself. Every time you see or feel something shift, your belief in your ability to make change in your life grows.

What a wonderful gift to give yourself. You are empowering yourself to become the best of you by letting go of what is not the truth of you. It is my deep honour to share this work with you and to guide you back to yourself. To me it is the greatest gift to give anyone – to support them in their journey to finding real love – the love of self.

We Are One

I dance with the eagle as my mind's eye
soars over the land.
I vibrate with the Spirits of the Earth and I
know that we are connected.
I am the eagle.
I am the blade of grass swaying in the
breeze.
I am the water rushing over rocks to meet
again in the great ocean.
I am the heartbeat of all life as it pulses ever
closer to God.
I am your brethren.
Feel me dance upon your Soul and recognize
that We Are One.

Chapter Ten - I Did It and So Can You!

As we come to the conclusion of this book there is something that I want you to remember. When I started doing this releasing work I was 56 years old, unemployed, living on my own, with no savings what so ever. Despite all of that I trusted that the universe was leading me in the right direction.

By choosing to have faith every day that my life was improving instead of falling apart, I recreated my experience from one of hardship to joy, and sometimes even magic. Notice I used the word 'choosing'. We create our lives with our attitudes and our thoughts. The beginning of making my life more positive was to make the decision to be positive in my thoughts. I simply was not willing to fall into fear.

Because of that, my life showed me something I had not seen before. It was very evident that my emotional choices were reflected in my life experience. So often we are reacting from fear without even realizing it. That is why it is so important to look at what your life is showing you and use that to honestly look at what may be the cause of what you see. If it's not attractive then what do you need to clear it and turn it around?

When we create from a place of fear what we get is not pretty! I know that from experience. In the year 2010, I was living in a house where I shared the expenses with my roommate. On my birthday of that year he announced that he was moving out in two weeks, leaving me with all the bills. We had no written contract that would protect me.

Panic! I finally found a new roommate who, a few months later, stole money from me and moved out not long afterward. (Did I mention I had money issues?) I moved into that house in a state of fear and look what I created. As I said, not pretty. I am telling you this so that you know that I have walked my talk in this process. I pulled myself out of those fearful experiences into a life where things flow and opportunities fall into my lap and life just keeps getting better.

After the determination to stay positive no matter what was showing up in my life experience, the next key factor in turning my life around was clearing the hidden beliefs that were impacting my thoughts. The more I worked on releasing limiting, unconscious beliefs, the more I would recognize when I was feeling something connected to fear.

It can be hard to see our own limitations. I found that, any time I was worried about something, it was a clear indication that there was an underlying belief that needed to be released. The more we do that, the clearer we become. Let's go back to that stone wall.

As children we build up the wall to protect ourselves. This, of course, continues into adulthood. Every time we feel vulnerable we place another stone on the wall to protect our sensitive hearts.

As we come to do this work and tear the wall down, we have to start at the top, with the last stone that was placed. We can't reach into the middle of a stone wall and pull out a stone. The stones on top are too heavy. We have to tear the wall down by removing the stones at the top – the most recent ones to be placed there.

The more clearing work we do, the deeper we get, closer to the core of our protection – our 'stuff'. Therefore, the more we clear, the lighter we become. As this happens, it is easier to notice things when they feel out of alignment. As long as we are paying attention, it becomes easier to see what is coming up to be cleared.

In this process it is important to be aware of our thoughts. If our minds are spinning, running thought after thought without consciously knowing what they are, we will not recognize when something appears that is of fear. By the time I stepped into the releasing work I had a good awareness of my thoughts.

Because of that, I could easily identify when my mind was moving toward worry or recognize a body sensation that was a reaction to something. That allowed me to easily realize what was coming up to be cleared. Another way of identification is to be aware of our feelings.

Whenever we feel guilty, or sad, or angry, or worried, we can be sure that there is an opportunity there to clear something that is limiting our faith that all is love. It is important to use these moments to keep clearing. Remember, life is always offering up opportunities for more growth!

Dedicating all of 2012 to healing was one of the best decisions I ever made in my life. A year might seem like a long time until you look over the last five or ten years of your life and discover that you carried the same worries, the same anguish, the same struggles through all those years.

When you look at it that way, one year dedicated to healing and releasing with the potential to turn your life around, doesn't seem like a long time at all. One year of focused intent that equals the rest of your life being more joyful and peaceful seems like a great investment to me.

And there is nothing saying that your commitment has to be a full year. Just be sure you don't lose focus after a couple of weeks and then forget about doing the clearing work. That will not be enough time to make it a practice to release what is holding you back and step into what you are becoming.

I suggest the intention to be doing this work for the rest of your life. Like I said before, it becomes joyful after a while. You see a troubling situation as an opportunity to become even lighter and happier as you lift one more stone off the wall of protection that keeps you from fully shining your heart light out into the world!

If you do releasing work and, between every clearing, focus on what is not working in your life, you will continue to get more of what is not working in your life. As you clear, inevitably, you would release more and more of your fears. But, if you were still focused on fearful thoughts, you would simply be inviting more of what doesn't work into your life.

That would give you more to be fearful about and you would create new beliefs that would not be leading to a life of bliss and joy. By consciously keeping your thoughts on what is working for you, you will attract more of what is working. This way, when you clear something, you are not creating some new limitation to fill its place.

That is why we must integrate who we are becoming and allow ourselves to resonate with the person we are in our fullness. Stay focused on the positive. Do not let that falter. Continually ask yourself, "Is this a thought coming from fear or love?" Every day wake up looking for what you would like to have in your life. And every time you see it, say 'yes', I have that in my life. Great! That attitude was the biggest change I made in my life and the beginning of me pulling my life out of struggle and into ease and grace.

I have shared many tools with you to support you in making the journey into a life of abundance and grace. Along the way in my work I created The Release Technique, which is difficult to share. It is a method of going into the subconscious to discover what is waiting to be released and then clearing it with my connection to the Divine.

It is a powerful method of releasing subconscious beliefs and discovering where they originated. They are then released and the shifts are immediately apparent in your life experience.

Like I said, the more you release, the lower the wall becomes and your heart feels safer to be the full expression of you in the world. The lower the wall, the more we love ourselves. The more we love ourselves, the more beautiful a life we create. It is the opposite of creating from fear.

When we create our lives from a place of loving the self, we allow true love, support, kindness, ease, grace, joy and magic to be our experience. It is what I wish for you all. We are meant to be living our Divine Expression in this world. We have come here not to be punished by a life of hardship, but to be in joy, celebrating life and creatively expressing all that we are without hesitation.

Not many of us are truly living that way. It has been a harsh journey. For sensitive souls, we often had to check out in a sense in order to be here at all. It is time to come back. It is time to create heaven on earth. It is time to empower yourself and find your joy – your bliss.

It won't happen by wishing and hoping. It happens with a clear mental attitude, a willingness to look into the shadows and a determination to turn your life around. If you would like support in your journey I would be glad to help. You can learn more about my work and experience some of my clearing work at the links at the end of this book.

It is by finding peace within ourselves that we can create a peaceful world. When the Divine essence of Love is allowed to fill our souls, there is nothing but peace, and the desire to be an expression of that Love – for all to feel.

It is my sincere intent that this book leads you to the place where you feel the Divinity of your Soul flowing in and around you; where your heart expands into the infinite blessings of creation that you so deserve. As we grow together there is great potential to create a world where love abounds and the earth is filled with joy. May it be so.

About the Author

Rashana lives in the beautiful province of Nova Scotia, Canada. She is an Intuitive Counselor, Channeler, Reiki Master, Certified Hypnotherapist, Sound Healer and the Creator of Rashana Sound Essences. She is a beautiful soul who presents her messages with love and compassion.

She channels the higher Beings of Light, including Ascended Masters, The Council of Nine and her over-soul. Rashana has appeared on national television, several radio shows and in front of large audiences. She has recorded 2 CDs and just completed her third book.

Her passion at this time is to empower others on their journey using channeling, sound healing and her most recent offering, The Freedom Release Technique, which she created to help her clients clear limiting beliefs that hold them back from the life of their dreams.

Please feel free to go to www.rashana.ca to get the book "Healing with Love – Messages for the New Earth" for free and find out more about the other books, CD's and other products on offer.

www.ingramcontent.com/pod-product-compliance
Lightning Source LLC
LaVergne TN
LVHW051151080426
835508LV00021B/2577